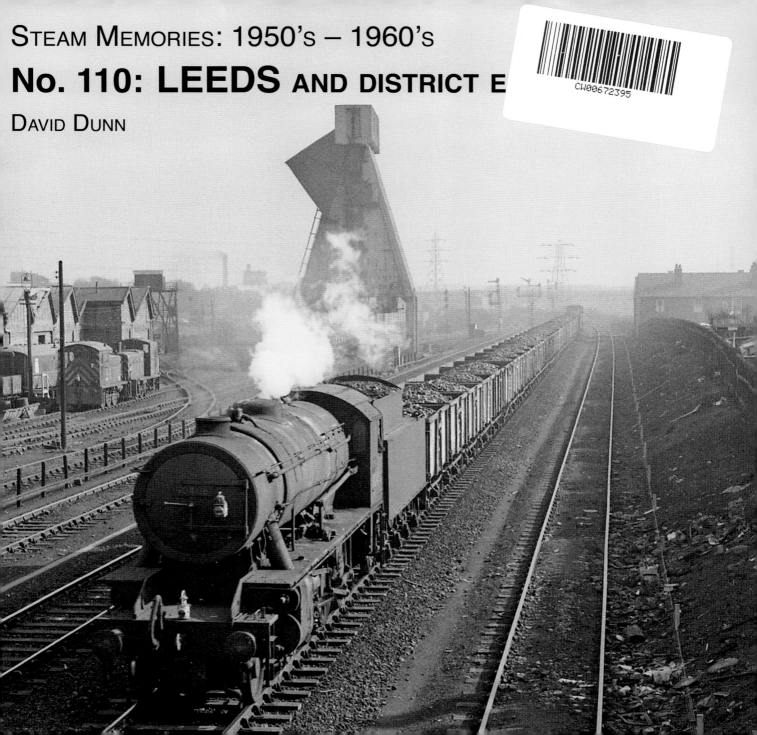

STEAM MEMORIES: 1950's – 1960's

No. 110: LEEDS AND DISTRICT E

DAVID DUNN

Copyright Book Law Publications 2019
ISBN 978-1-913049-08-9

INTRODUCTION

Part 2 of the Leeds area engine sheds album completes the duo of 80-page tomes illustrating the fourteen motive power depots which made up the 55 and 56 group sheds in the latter days of BR steam. This particular album contains views of Bradford Hammerton Street, Low Moor, Manningham, Sowerby Bridge, Mirfield, Huddersfield, Wakefield, and Royston. Of course we also threw in another image of Normanton as promised but we have so many more illustrations to offer showing all the sheds and their eclectic variety of locomotives.

David Dunn, June 2019.

(*cover*) **Wakefield, where else? It is 1962 and the Dub-Dees have certainly taken over.** *W.Coulson*.

(*previous page*) **With just months left before proceedings regarding steam motive power come to a halt, WD No.90406 runs north past Wakefield motive power depot with a long loaded coal train on 18th March 1967.** *Ken Groundwater (ARPT)*.

Printed and bound by The Amadeus Press, Cleckheaton, West Yorkshire
First published in the United Kingdom by Book Law Publications, 382 Carlton Hill, Nottingham, NG4 1JA

BRADFORD (Bowling Junction, aka Hammerton Street) 37C, 56G, 55F

The former Great Northern engine shed at Bradford Bowling Junction was the third such motive power depot built by the company in Bradford. Being the last, it was, as usual, the largest and was opened in March 1883 replacing a four road structure at nearby Adolphus Street. Bowling Junction shed, also known as Bowling, and more recently by its latest moniker as Hammerton Street, comprised ten roads covered by a northlight roof, and also its western side a two-road repair shop with a 25-ton capacity overhead crane for lifting engines was provided. For the next seventy-five years it housed an allocation which was purely GNR then gradually from 1923 elements of the LNER Standard classes started to arrive and then from 1948 BR Eastern Region influence saw various types joining the fleet. However, in 1955 the northlight roof – or what was left of it – was replaced by a BR standard design roof constructed from concrete modules and components, some on site others at BR Civil Engineers workshops. In 1958 steam was ousted from the depot and Hammerton Street as it was then known became one of BR's first all-diesel depots which mainly housed multiple units used for the local services and the cross-Pennine routes. A small number of diesel shunters were also allocated. The image above shows one of Gresley's N1 tank engines in the shed yard alongside a water column on Sunday 5th May 1957. This was amongst the last of the steam fleet here. *Clive Allen (ARPT)*.

3

J50 No.68922 was one of the final GNR locomotive designs and altogether – along with detail differences – some 102 of them were constructed by both the GN and later by the LNER. They were always a large part of Bowling Junction's stud with no less than twenty-one of them allocated when British Railways came into being. It is worth looking at the allocation of locomotives on that first day of 1948 because it reveals how much Bradford relied on tank engines to carry out its numerous duties. Besides the aforementioned J50s, there was a group of four N5s which had origins back in the days of the Manchester, Sheffield & Lincolnshire Railway. The 0-6-2Ts, or to be more specific two of them, had arrived in 1935 and that pair was quickly joined by two more. However, they were gone during the early 1950s as the run-down of the depot's steam fleet started. Besides the N5s, the GN was further represented by fourteen N1s which completed the tank engine complement. On that first day of BR Bradford had just forty-nine locomotives allocated which when you remove the thirty-nine tanks, you are left with just ten tender engines for the long-distant work. Those ten comprised a couple of Thompson B1s, a Q4 eight-coupled goods engine – No.3217 – and seven J6. Although none were allocated, Gresley and Peppercorn Pacifics were regular visitors to Bowling Junction to use the repair facility, mainly the wheel-drop; note the A3 behind No.68922. *Clive Allen (ARPT).*

A long standing resident of Bradford Bowling shed, J6 No.64170 was there during the final full year when steam motive power was still welcome. This 5th May 1957 image shows the 0-6-0 alongside an LNER 8-wheel tender which was couple to that unidentified A3. On the right of the picture is part of the concrete coaling plant which was erected in 1937 as part of the LNER's cost cutting exercise which cost £9,000 at Bradford alone. Back to the J6, this particular locomotive was the first of what became the LNER J6 class and was the first GNR 0-6-0 goods engine to be superheated and in August 1911 when it entered traffic, it was numbered 521. Initially shedded at Colwick, this 0-6-0 moved around the old GNR system during LNER times serving also at Leicester, Hornsey, Retford, Ardsley and even Neepsend the former GCR shed at Sheffield during WW2. It's first and only residency at Bradford Bowling started on 24th November 1946 and the engine moved away to Low Moor on 12th January 1958 along with the thirty-odd remaining steam engines. The DMUs had arrived. At Grouping Bradford could muster ninety engines on its roster; by 1931 this had reduced to seventy locomotives. The allocation kept falling as the 1948 figures above reveal. Bradford Hammerton Street aka Bowling Junction closed completely from 13th May 1984 its diesel units transferring to Leeds Neville Hill. *Clive Allen (ARPT).*

The south end of Huddersfield's six-road through shed with the two-road dead-end shed alongside. The date of the photograph is 6th July 1958 and Crewe South Cl.5 No.45000 is stabled ready to work home. Behind are the usual suspects found at 55G at this time, a couple of Fowler Cl.4MT tanks, and a WD 2-8-0. It will be noted that this corner of the old LMS was well catered for as regards the 'Austerity' 8F and Huddersfield could muster ten or so for most of the BR period. Indeed once BR was up and running the depot also had eight Stanier Cl.5s, five Hughes/Fowler 'Crab' 2-6-0, a 'Jubilee', a 7F 0-8-0, and half a dozen assorted ex-Lanky tanks. It was all a far-cry from September 1935 when the depot could boast just five locomotives of LMS origin – five 'Crabs' – with the rest of the stud made up of twenty-one former L&NWR and twenty-two ex-L&YR locomotives! Under BR Huddersfield's fortunes slowly ebbed away with twenty-six engines allocated in 1959 as opposed to forty-two at Nationalisation although eight of those were the 7F 0-8-0s of LMS origin, the 'Austin Sevens' with those small axleboxes! It was during WW2 that Huddersfield acquired its first Fowler Cl.4 tank No.2414; by the end of the LMS eleven of them graced the shed yard and six of those had the limousine cabs which gave the crews a modicum of protection whilst working 'over the tops' to Stockport in winter. *N.W.Skinner (ARPT)*.

Former BR 9F Crosti No.92021 was a Birkenhead engine on Saturday 26th March 1966 when this image was recorded at what might be regarded as the north end of the shed yard 55G – the original northlight roof was still covering the office, stores section – turned and serviced ready to work back west. The BR Standard 9Fs from Birkenhead were regular visitors to Huddersfield, mainly working through the town towards Leeds or Healey Mills but the occasional engine called in for refreshment. Mention earlier of the protection offered to crews whilst working over the Standedge route, when the Fowler 2-6-4Ts were first being used from Hillhouse. Most of the freight engines then were 0-8-0s of LMS and LNWR origin which offered minimum protection working boiler first. In tender-first running it was pure torture even with a tarpaulin tied down between cab and tender. Now these 2-10-0s! Open the window it's too hot in here! 120 years roughing it, ten years of comfort and then it was all change to those draughty diesels! *A.Ives (ARPT)*.

Another view of No.92021 being prepared for its next duty on 26th March 1966! There is still a nip in the air but not much else. By now the allocation is down to four Class 4MT tanks and eight WD 2-8-0s. That situation didn't change much until the final month of steam operations when the 'Austerities' worked virtually everything - which wasn't a lot by then; the final working off 55G was performed by one of the depot's WD 2-8-0s prior to closure on 2nd January 1967. This view taken from the footbridge spanning Hillhouse sidings reveals more of the original northlight roof over the stores section. Up to 1937 the whole shed was protected by these northlight roofs, a favourite of industrial undertakings during the 1880s. The design was fairly lightweight compared with the more traditional single pitched roofs then in use and so it was quickly adopted during the next three decades or so. It offered a means of getting daylight into the work areas and the glazed areas could be built so that there was no glare hence the name. Some were of course western lights, others eastern lights but few were southern lights. The LMS saw fit to renewal the northlight roofs because the one weakness was the pollution created by smoke along with all the pollutants therein. Note the use of a single water column at this end of the shed; none of that luxury of a column between every two roads here! *A.Ives (ARPT)*.

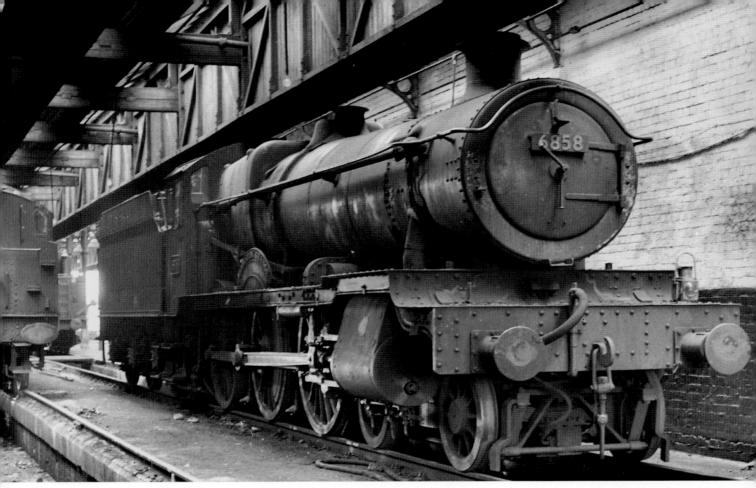

There are those of you who might well have already known about the following incident. There are those lucky enough to have witnessed the event and who relish telling the story to those who missed it all. On Saturday 15th August 1964 the Poole-Bradford Saturdays Only summer season express (1N72) pulled into Nottingham (Victoria) at 2.35 p.m. with the usual Western Region motive power at its head. It was normal practice to take the 'Grange' or 'Hall' off the train here and replace with basically anything that Annesley could supply – usually a Stanier Cl.5 or even a B1. However, on this day there was no replacement engine available and so the train engine 'Grange' No.6858 WOOLSTON GRANGE remained coupled to the train and the Annesley crew climbed aboard and took the 4-6-0 off to Sheffield. At Sheffield the left side cylinder cover apparently displaced a platform coping on the approach to Victoria station and because of that the NER relieving crew – from Low Moor shed – refused to take it over; Darnall as you've guessed had nothing to replace No.6858 either! A Locomotive Inspector stepped in and agreed to take the 'Grange' and 1N72 onto the next stop at Huddersfield. En route No.6858 damaged the timber platform at Denby Dale and Huddersfield became the final stop on the 4-6-0s destructive excursion to the north. The engine was stabled on Hillhouse shed for a number of days and here she was photographed whilst the authorities were still working out a route to get No.6858 safely back to the WR. Unfortunately, the cylinder cover which supposedly caused the mayhem was on the other side of the locomotive so we can't comment about any alleged damage. *Malcolm Foreman.*

An undated photograph of an incident at the eastern throat of the Hillhouse goods yard and although of a somewhat minor nature, the incident still required the services of one of the Running Department's large breakdown cranes to lift, part, and untangle a handful of wagons which decided on a 'get-together!' Attending to the needs of the crane is resident 0-6-0 saddletank No.51524 one of three ex-Lanky Aspinall 2F tanks (L&YR Class F16 which were 1891-1900 rebuilds of Barton-Wright six-coupled tender engines dating from 1876-87) which became BR property whilst allocated at 25B; the other two were Nos.11408 which moved onto Agecroft and was withdrawn in February 1962, and 11447 which transferred to Newton Heath before it got its BR number and became an early casualty being condemned in January 1957, albeit at least fifty-seven years old! No.51524 ended its days by the seaside at Fleetwood in September 1960 when that town had a fishing industry. This view is looking west towards the station with the Pennines on the horizon. We can see the mechanical coaling and ash plants provided by the LMS during the war years as the final part of a scheme authorised in 1934; the roof as already mentioned was renewed in 1937 as part of the same scheme. Which depot supplied the breakdown crane is unknown but it may well have been the Holbeck crane earning its keep. This area is now completely altered and you would be hard-pressed to imagine that a railway installation such as this existed here. *Ernie Brack collection.*

LOW MOOR 25F, 56F, 55J

Okay, some might say it's not the best view of an engine shed illustrated in this series but it is certainly interesting and gives a number of answers to what happened at this depot during the BR period especially. The date is 9th March 1958, and as you have already guessed by the turn-out of locomotives it was a Sunday. We can only see half of the depot from this vantage point at the rear south-western corner with the by now de-roofed portion of the shed prominent in its nakedness. Low Moor started out as a 12-road shed in 1888 with the usual coaling stage, turntable, and maintenance facilities for sixty-odd locomotives. On this date the gathering here consisted LMS standard locomotives of the Cl.8, Cl.5, 4F, 4MT tanks, alongside ex-LNER J50 0-6-0Ts, J39 0-6-0s, and earlier 0-6-0 tender engines of Great Northern Railway origin. It was certainly full with sixty-odd engines on shed and up on the post-war numbers entering Nationalisation which was just forty-odd engines. The reason for the increase was the influx from the closure of Hammerton Street shed on 12th January last. The coaling plant in the distance was a product of the LMS era as was the ash plant. If any shed reviewed in these albums could claim to be cosmopolitan it would have been Low Moor. Just about the middle period of the LMS era before Stanier's engines started to make a mark away from the WCML sheds, in September 1935 for instance, Low Moor had sixty-four engines on the books. These consisted: 3 LMS 2P 4-4-0; 5 LMS 4P 4-4-0; 4 LMS 'Crab' 2-6-0; 1 LMS 4F 0-6-0; 2 LMS Cl.5 4-6-0; 2 ex-LNW 5F/6F 0-8-0; 3 ex-LNW 4P 4-6-0; 6 ex-LYR/LMS 5P 4-6-0; 16 ex-LYR 2P/3P 2-4-2T; 4 ex-LYR 2F 0-6-0ST; 13 ex-LYR 3F 0-6-0; 3 ex-LYR 6F 0-8-0; 2 ex-LYR 7F 0-8-0. Thirteen classes and then further sub-classes within those. That is a lot of spares! *W.R.E.Lewis (ARPT).*

11

A nice view of the shed yard on a damp day during September 1967 with only resident B1 No.61306 and Hammerton Street based 204 h.p. 0-6-0DM D2102 identified. By now there were less than a dozen operational steam locomotives allocated to the depot with twice as many withdrawn examples dotted about the place. Having spent all of its life working from the Hull sheds at Botanic Gardens or Dairycoates, the B1 was a late arrival at Low Moor having transferred from the latter shed on 25th June last. By some co-incidence D2102 was also ex-Dairycoates having arrived in Bradford on 21st January 1967. The B1 was withdrawn on the last day of September, a Saturday, whilst the depot closed officially two days afterwards on 2nd October 1967 – a Monday, always on a Monday! Note the 55J shed plate on No.61306, Low Moor's new coding from August 1967 to closure – how many weeks?! No.61306 went into preservation whilst the Doncaster-built 0-6-0DM was sold to a scrapyard in Kettering in 1976. *D.R. Dunn collection.*

Inside the shed during a late evening in September 1967 with 55J plates prominent amongst the residents; well two of them anyway! During this final month of operations the ex-LMS Cl.4 tank engines still working – most of them were recent transfers in and their last shed and date of transfer is posted alongside – comprised the following: 42072 ex Holbeck 8/67; 42141 ex Royston 5/67; 42152 ex Holbeck 8/67; 42251 ex Tebay 4/67; 42283 ex Trafford Park 4/67; 42616 ex Birkenhead 5/67; 42689 ex Holbeck 8/67. During 1967 a further nine of them had been condemned. *Maurice Burns.*

The opening illustration revealed what was to be seen from the east side of the former west wall of the shed whilst this view – albeit at a different date – shows what was stored on that single road alongside that west wall and used for storing locomotives awaiting shops or for scrap. The date is a rather fine 29th December 1958 and ex-L&Y 'A' Class 3F 0-6-0 No.52413 is kissed by the morning sun as it awaits attention. This was one of the class rebuilt with a Belpaire boiler and extended smokebox. As things turned out the 0-6-0 was sorted with a new buffer and sent on transfer to Sowerby Bridge where it worked until withdrawn in November 1962. *N.W.Skinner (ARPT).*

(*opposite, top*) No nameplates, everything else intact: 'Jubilee' No.45581 BIHAR AND ORISSA visits from Farnley Junction on 17th July 1966. This must have been one of the last duties the 4-6-0 performed because it was withdrawn just days later. The full extent of the terraced row of railway servant housing can be gleaned from this image; not the ornate brickwork and the two end properties which were each of three storeys. *N.W.Skinner (ARPT).* (*opposite*) Recently acquired Cl.5 No.44951 stands near the ash plant on 19th August 1962. The 4-6-0 had transferred from Wakefield in June. This engine was one of those which could not settle anywhere it seems. During its lifetime it was shedded at Low Moor three times totalling some thirteen years. It moved from Low Moor to Wakefield during December 1966 but was withdrawn immediately; the chances are, it never left 56F and was condemned before it could be moved. *C.J.B.Sanderson (ARPT).*

14

One of the J39s which found a home at Low Moor resides at the buffer stops erected when the old shed roof was removed in 1948 and this, the western half of the shed, was left exposed to the elements. No.64817 had spent all of its life working in what was the former North Eastern Railway area and 56F was its final posting on 25th January 1959, ex-Sunderland. Attending Cowlairs works in February 1962, the 0-6-0 was condemned there on following 29th March and subsequently cut up. This view from 11th April 1960 shows the J39 alongside one of the depots' WD 2-8-0s which frequented the shed from June 1956 onwards; altogether seventeen 'Austerities' were shedded at Low Moor up to July 1967 and two of them were condemned at the shed. *A.R.Thompson collection.*

A conglomeration of locomotive types gathered in this 19th August 1962 image captured at the rear of the section of the shed minus a roof. The amenities building over which the camera scanned this part of the depot in the opening illustration can just be seen above the Ivatt Cl.2 tanks in the left background. Prominent are a couple of Low Moor's acquired J50 0-6-0Ts from Hammerton Street's closure and found to be useful little engines and therefore kept for a while. Amongst this lot are B1s, J39s, J50s, Fowler Cl.4s, Ivatt Cl.2s. and others. Mention was made above of the cosmopolitan nature of Low Moor in the mid-LMS period. The same could be said for the mid-BR steam period when even more classes and locomotives served the depot in early 1959 thus: 4 ex-LMS Cl.2 2-6-2T; 1 ex-LMS Cl.2 2-6-0; 4 ex-LMS Cl.3F 0-6-0T; 12 ex-LMS Cl.4 2-6-4T; 1 ex-LMS Cl.4 2-6-0; 1 ex-LMS Cl.4 0-6-0; 11 ex-LMS Cl.5 4-6-0; 3 ex-LMS Cl.8F 2-8-0; 1 ex-MR 3F 0-6-0; 2 ex-LYR 3F 0-6-0; 2 ex-WD 8F 2-8-0; 6 B1 4-6-0; 3 J6 0-6-0; 9 J39 0-6-0; 10 J50 0-6-0T. Then the clear-outs! Of course we have not listed every class which worked from 56F in BR days but Stanier 3MT 2-6-2T Nos.40074, 40147, 40155 and 40190 come to mind (four of these engines Nos.190-193 started their LMS careers at Low Moor in November 1937 and most of them served the shed through wartime); then the 'Jubilees' 45565 and 45694 (again this class had been beforehand when the LMS sent new Nos.5724, 5725, and 5726 in September 1936 for a few months only!); then the 'Scots' 46109, 46113, 46117, 46130, and 46145 which arrived in September 1961 but three had gone to Mirfield in December whilst the other two went to Holbeck in June 1962 in time for withdrawal. The LMS period is a whole different story again and can wait for another appropriate time. *C.J.B.Sanderson (ARPT).*

Another view inside the shed but now daylight has returned enough to allow the photographer to record this view of resident Cl.5 No.44693 in 1962. Besides the locomotive, we can see the new parts of the rebuilt shed albeit looking anything but new with soot and goodness knows what having changed their concrete shading since the job was done a dozen or so years beforehand. The original shed building incorporated a set of hydraulically powered shearlegs and these were carefully included into the rebuilt shed with the roof section around them modified to fit; one set of legs belonging to the appliance can be seen on the left rising into the roof. On the right is the original eastern wall of the 1888 shed building which was incorporated into the rebuilding. Note those hefty personal lockers. *Malcolm Foreman.*

This image has been included to illustrate the route taken by visitors to the shed and the steps from where the opening image was recorded on film. The view was caught that same morning and it appears to have captured many otherwise forgotten corners of Low Moor engine shed and the surrounding residential properties, many of the latter being former Company servant dwellings. The 2P without a buffer! That was No.50855 which came to Low Moor during the summer of 1956 from Bolton but returned there a few months after this March 1958 photograph was taken. It was withdrawn on arrival at 26C. *W.R.E.Lewis (ARPT).*

Before we leave Low Moor, mention must be made that this engine shed was – if you didn't already know – a former Lancashire & Yorkshire railway establishment which kept hold of many of its original complement right up to the North Eastern Region take over. Even then a couple of die-hards seemingly refused to move out but eventually they went to Sowerby Bridge in the early 1960s; Nos.52413 and 52461 were both withdrawn at Sowerby Bridge in November and October 1962 respectively! When BR came into being Low Moor could muster eighteen ex-Lanky engines from its forty-seven steeds but this figure reduced over the next decade to just two. Even with transfers in and out though Low Moor sent twenty-four four and six-coupled tank and tender engines for scrap during that first ten years. Here on the site of the original northlight shed which was not re-roofed we see 2P 2-4-2T No.50859 and an unidentified 'A' class 0-6-0 stabled on Sunday 21st August 1955. The 2P was withdrawn from Low Moor during the following November. *F.W.Hampson collection (ARPT)*.

Five Ivatt Cl.4 2-6-0s stood around the turntable pit at Manningham on an unknown date in 1966. By this time the allocation at 55F was down to less than a dozen steam locomotives and any diesel shunters were out-stationed from Hammerton Street. The roundhouse here was opened by the Midland Railway in 1872 and was of the standard design for the square roundhouses adopted by the company. One slight deviation from the normal design, and showing the ongoing evolution with shed designs and construction, was the use of full deep girders which spanned the whole length of the building on either side of the turntable. Earlier sheds used the lattice girder beams but ornamental function was slowly being removed from shed designs on the Midland. The smoke individual troughs were of a BR design and were installed by the North Eastern Region shortly after they took over the former LMS engine sheds in the West Riding. What of the locomotives stabled? Left to right, they were: Nos.43074, 43030, 43135, 43054 and 43050 of which only three were operational. *D.R. Dunn collection*.

Another internal view but at an earlier date – Sunday 8th April 1962 – with a bit of balance to the locomotive content. On the left is Cl.4 tank No.42072 one of the shed's pool of reliable 2-6-4Ts which were allocated to virtually the end. The next steam locomotive is Ivatt Cl.4 No.43074 which looks much better here and was actually a newcomer to the shed just a few months beforehand. In between the steamers was a solitary but unidentified 350 h.p. 0-6-0DE shunter. Now at this time Manningham had four of these useful units allocated: D3457, D3656, D3657, and D3658. None of them came new to 55F but the last three came all together in June 1958 from Stourton and remained at Manningham until sent away during the autumn of 1964 to Farnley Junction, Neville Hill and Farnley Junction respectively. D3457 arrived in June 1959 from Hammerton Street and departed back there in July 1964. *N.W.Skinner (ARPT).*

Four more Ivatts in various states but nevertheless some serious lumps of metal: Nos.43140, 43135, and 43051. The date is 17th July 1966, another reasonable summer but this crowd were all approaching their own winters. *N.W.Skinner (ARPT)*.

A view of the shed looking north from Queens Road bridge, which spanned the main line from Shipley, and the platforms of the erstwhile Manningham passenger station. 'Britannia' No.70031 is inching along the main towards Forster Square station with a parcels train as locomotives go about their business on the shed yard. It looks as though the demolition gang are at work on the station whilst enthusiasts take advantage of the deserted platforms in this scene from 29th April 1967. The station which was opened by the Midland Railway on 17th February 1868 had been closed by BR two years beforehand on 22nd March 1965. *A.R.Thompson (ARPT)*.

They looked the business even when filthy, neglected, nameless but alive with fire and steam; No.70031 BYRON alongside the coaling stage at Manningham 29th April 1967. *A.R.Thompson (ARPT).*

The off-centre entrance to Manningham roundhouse on 29th April 1967 some ninety-five years after it was built. Note the use of local stone for the construction of the shed, one of the few Midland roundhouses which used materials other than bricks. This was the only entry/exit for the roundhouse but it seemingly sufficed. *A.R.Thompson (ARPT).*

Former Lanky 2P 2-4-2T No.50636 was one of a dozen such engines allocated to Manningham during the early days of BR but only half that number were on the books in LMS days. As BR found its feet the ex-L&YR engines became quite popular in these parts and the Manningham sub-shed at Ilkley was home to the class for many years. The sudden popularity of these 2-4-2Ts was because of the repatriation of the four former Caledonian 0-4-4T Nos.15130, 15169, 15192 and 15227 north of the border shortly after Nationalisation during summer 1948. The ex-CR tanks were loaned during a crucial period in 1947. The Ilkley services had been dieselised totally by 1959 and the last of the L&Y tanks moved away to Lancashire and oblivion at Horwich during the autumn of that year. *F.W.Hampson (ARPT)*.

Stored Lanky 2P No.50795 stood on the site of the preparation area of the old timber-built shed on the south-east corner of the depot on 29th March 1959. This was the last of the L&YR types here and it was withdrawn during November 1959 then taken to Gorton works for breaking up. Its ex-Midland stablemate is 3F 0-6-0 No.43784 which was withdrawn in 1960 but had seen little work for a couple of years. *Ian Falcus*.

A final but deserving view of the inside of Manningham shed on Saturday 29th April 1967 with a group of four Cl.4 tank engines ready for work. A Drewry 204 h.p. 0-6-0DM hides amongst the hot metal. Besides the 350 h.p. DE shunters, Manningham was also home for five of the smaller diesel-mechanical shunters thus: D2044 which arrived from Percy Main on 19th September 1964 but moved to Hammerton Street at closure on 29th April 1967; D2065 came from York on 24th October 1964 and then moved on to Neville Hill on 19th June 1965; D2071 came from Hammerton St. on 21st July 1964 and left just before closure going to Gateshead; D2102 came from Dairycoates during the third week of January 1967 and went to Hammerton St. after Manningham shed had been cleared out on 14th May 1967; D2161 was another from York coming to Bradford on 14th November 1964 and then transferring to Hammerton Street on 22nd April 1967. *A.R.Thompson (ARPT)*.

A bleak Bradford Manningham on 9th March 1958 with a smattering of snow on the ground – it looks as though it was the remnants of a larger fall which was now melting. This was sixty years ago but the shed was less than ten years away from closure. Bradford was still expanding then and residential properties are shoulder-to-shoulder on the left of the image whilst the right background reveals open land on the higher areas of the city. To add to the bleakness, it will be noted that the few trees have all been shaped by the wind; even here on the eastern slopes of the Pennines the prevailing winds come from the west. Back to the railway infrastructure and we must mention the four-road straight shed – built of wood and with a northlight roof – which stood on the east side of the yard here, its locomotive entrance marked by servicing pits which were still in situ whilst the shed roads proper have been all but covered by the coal stack. The shed apparently became redundant in the early years of WW2 and was demolished sometime during the conflict; it had opened in late 1887. The roundhouse frontage is obscured by the coaling shed which was itself extended at an unknown date to give it two coaling faces to cater for increased usage. Manningham engine shed closed at the end of April 1967 but as local observers will agree, the facilities were used by visiting steam locomotives for some time afterwards; Kingmoor shed still had some healthy parcels traffic with Bradford and it was some time before 12A stopped sending their Pacifics on those turns. *W.R.E.Lewis (ARPT).*

Just to make sure! An enthusiast searches the motion on Stanier 8F No.48774 looking for numbers to prove that the locomotive is or isn't what it appears. The 8F was one of three – 48773-48775 – purchased by BR from the War Department in 1957 and was formerly WD501; ex-LMS 8246. No.48774 had arrived back in the United Kingdom from service in the Middle East with a number of other Stanier 8Fs which were mainly refurbished at Derby for the WD and put back into military service and various installations in the UK. BR purchased thirty-nine ex-WD Stanier 8Fs altogether, most reverting to their firmer LMS numbers. Our subject did not however not only receive a new number in the Stanier 8F range but prior to entering traffic was given the number 90743 and then immediately after No.90734; No.48773 would have become 90733 if this scheme had been adhered too. The entry to traffic for the trio was at Polmadie in September 1957 where in December 1962 they were withdrawn only to be re-instated in January to help out during the extreme winter when diesel locomotives were failed left, right, and centre. With the winter safely out of the way Scottish Region decided in June 1963 to withdrawn them once again! The following October all three were re-instated again but at Kingmoor. From 12A the sisters were split up with No.48774 transferring to Speke Junction in May 1964 and being withdrawn there for the third and final time during July 1965. The others had moved on to the likes of Lostock Hall or Rose Grove and both of them were still operational at the end in August 1968. Although undated, this image must have been recorded when No.48774 was on the books at Speke Junction where they failed to give it a shed plate. *Ian H. Hodgson (ARPT).*

31

Ex-L&YR 2P No.50777 and Cl.4 No.42639 in circa 1953 when Sowerby Bridge was still part of the London Midland Region coded 25E. We have no date for this illustration but it is probably winter or at least one of the cooler seasons either side because the engine still has its train heating pipe attached and the five visitors in the distance are wrapped up for cold weather shed bashing. This view shows the new brickwork of the shed rebuilding – 1952-53 – sitting atop the original stone walls of 1887 the year the six-road shed was opened to replace an earlier shed which had operated nearby since 1857. *K.H.Cockerill (ARPT).*

We saw this 'A' Class in dire straits at Low Moor in December 1958 but it's typical of many illustrations in that they look worse than things actually are. It is nearly four years on and No.52413 looks in fine fettle in this 8th April 1962 image looking north from the turntable road. It is another Sunday and the weather has turned out nice again! The 3F never did get one of the new BR crests applied on its tender to replace the original lion and wheel emblem as it was called into Horwich, withdrawn and then cut up in November 1962. Clinging to the hillside opposite, residential properties of all types rub shoulders with engineering concerns. *N.W.Skinner (ARPT).*

'Jinty' No.47508 waits at the coaling stage on that chilly Sunday 9th March 1958. This 3F 0-6-0T and its sister 47509 spent all of their BR careers working from Sowerby Bridge; they also had No.47510 for company but that 3F moved on shortly after Nationalisation. The eagle-eyed will have noted the wrong facing BR crest on the tank side. *W.R.E.Lewis (ARPT)*.

(*opposite, top*) In February 1958 Fowler Cl.4 No.42405 transferred from Mirfield to Sowerby Bridge but by the winter of 1961 the 2-6-4T was redundant so went into store in the goods yard. By 8th April 1962 when this image was recorded, No.42405 was showing the signs of the enforced rest. DMUs were basically the downfall of these Class 4MT engines and this part of the world was knee deep in green units taking over everything it seemed. In November 1962 this engine transferred to Darlington – its first foray off the old Central Division since new in September 1933 – where it ended its day some two years later. *N.W.Skinner (ARPT)*.

(*opposite*) Now here is an unusual story of an event which didn't happen too often but when it did heads were being scratched. Ivatt Cl.4 No.43126 was allocated to Sowerby Bridge from September 1957 to July 1959 when it was transferred to Heaton. Here on Sunday 25th September 1960 the 2-6-0 is stabled with a couple of WD 2-8-0s as large as life and wearing a new 56E shed plate! The Cl.4 should have been stabled at Sunderland its new home after transferring from Gateshead. So, the question arises as to why it was languishing at Sowerby Bridge more than a year after leaving the shed? Note also the ex-works condition and the correct facing BR crest. *F.W.Hampson (ARPT)*.

35

The LMS 7F 'Austin Seven' 0-8-0 was one of those locomotive types you expected to see at 25E and if you had visited the shed between April 1955 and July 1956 you would probably have met No.49552 here. No.49554 was another which was there at the same time. During WW2 the shed had ten of them allocated and they were the mainstay of the heavy freight motive power in the valley. A similar number of six-coupled 3F and 4F made up the other main-line goods engines. When BR came into being the number of 7Fs allocated was eight and gradually that number fell as more WD 2-8-0s became available to work the depots freight traffic. In BR times twelve of the 0-8-0s served the depot but never all together and usually for just short periods. No.49552 transferred to Newton Heath in July 1956 and was withdrawn on arrival! *P.J. Robinson.*

BR Standard Cl.2 No.78012 was a visitor from Bolton in this undated view which shows the twelve-years old 2-6-0 to be in less than peak external condition. This engine had spent its first ten years working from various shed in the North Eastern Region but in December 1964 it was transferred from Tweedmouth to Gorton. Like a hot potato it was passed from shed to shed, each establishment finding it more difficult to employ such locomotives for any given time. It transferred to Bolton in August 1966 from Trafford Park where it has languished for a year doing next to nothing. Its time at Bolton – 9K as we are reminded by the painted version of the information found on shed plates – was curtailed in May 1967 when, along with its classmates at that depot – Nos.78007, 78013, 78023, 78044, and 78062 – the Cl.2 was withdrawn. At Lostock Hall a similar cull took place when Nos.78020, 78021, 78037, and 78041 were also withdrawn bringing to extinction the BR Standard Cl.2 tender engine. *Gordon Turner/GD/ARPT.*

The view of the engine shed and its environs from the high ground bordering the rear of the depot on Sunday 9th March 1958. As can be seen, the adjacent goods yard, or certain sidings therein were utilised by the motive power department for stabling locomotives awaiting works or simply put into seasonal storage. Only two locomotives are identified by their numbers: resident 2P No.50777 which was withdrawn at the end of the forthcoming summer timetable, and another resident, 3F No.52399 which was about to be condemned at the end of the month but the log shows 2P No.50818 and WD No.90113 were also in the dump. On show were four of the depot's WD 'Austerity' 2-8-0s, a visiting Ivatt Class 4 and a couple of Sowerby's 3F 0-6-0Ts. It was bleak but that is the nature of winter in this part of the country and in 1958 Sunday's were generally bleak anyway all over the country. *W.R.E.Lewis (ARPT).*

Birkenhead 9Fs 2-10-0s were daily visitors to Mirfield and former Crosti fitted No.92023 gets ready to depart from the shed and make its way to Healey Mills yard to pick-up a westbound freight but has to wait for a Stanier 8F to come on shed first. It was usual for Birkenhead crews to work eastbound trains as far as Stockport where Edgeley crews would take-over for the trip 'over the tops' into Yorkshire; a return trip would nicely seal a shift assuming everything went right. The livery worn by the 9F was the 'end-of-steam' buff which most locomotives started to wear during the 1960s and this 26th March 1966 image shows the engine just as it was withdrawn twenty months hence. This particular 9F spent just over two years in store after its temporary withdrawal with its Crosti problems; some of them spent even longer laid-up. During 1955 No.92023 spent six months at Rugby Testing Station being evaluated and then, as a prelude of things to come, it was sent on loan to Carlisle Kingmoor where many of the class would end their operational lives during the mid-Sixties. *A.Ives (ARPT).*

On that same Saturday in March 1966 the photographer was able to capture this Stanier 8F which had just finished being coaled at the manual coaling stage. The image is a study in locomotive design and building architecture with the filthy NBL-built 8F showing off what was certainly a masterpiece of British locomotive engineering. Built in July 1942 and put into traffic at Toton, the 2-8-0 transferred from the East Midlands to Normanton in 1950 and remained in Yorkshire for the rest of its life. It had been at Mirfield since November 1960 and you would have thought that a shed plate was fitted then – perhaps it was – but the crude rendering in white paint of 56D was all that the 8F was going to get from this date. No.48202 transferred to Wakefield in January 1967 and was condemned six months later. Meanwhile let's have a look at the stage which was topped by that cast-iron ornate water tank. The structure was built using a mixture of stone and brick with fortress type walls to support the massive weight of the tank before that mass of water was included! Water levels are evident in the 8Fs tender which has yet to be topped up, and the water tank above which was half full, or is that half empty? *A.Ives (ARPT).*

Now during the 1960s the ebb and flow of change on BR as regards motive power was constant. It got to the point where surprise was no longer considered. Such were the out-of-the-ordinary events that we began to get used to them and as for keeping up with them, well that was another matter! However, one event which did occur and which raised many eyebrows was the allocation of six B16/1s in December 1960 from their usual haunts to Mirfield. Although technically still within the NE Region, Mirfield was in the former L&Y the LMS and LMR patch acquired through boundary changes five years previously. Our illustration shows No.61447 the last – numerically – of the B16/1 batch which arrived on 11th December 1960 to work coal trains and passenger services. The 4-6-0 is standing outside the shed in early summer 1961 with a sister engine for company. The other B16/1 were: Nos.61411 withdrawn 25th September 1961; 61412 same withdrawal date; 61413 ditto; 61414 ditto; 61416 withdrawn 12th May 1961. No.61447 was also condemned 25th September 1961. But the story doesn't end there. On 10th September 1961 five B16 Part 3s were drafted in to cover for the forthcoming withdrawal of the remaining B16/1s. Nos.61449 was eventually condemned at Mirfield on 3rd July 1963 whilst the other four B16/3s: 61461, 61464, 61468, and 61476 were all condemned en masse on 16th September 1963 – interesting times. Of course there were no electronic social networks then, the only news outlets were Trains Illustrated and Railway Magazine or the society journals such as the Railway Observer and SLS Journal but by the time you received any of those the events had usually passed. So, keeping an eye on as much as possible, listen to platform-end gossip, and keep your fingers crossed. But then, how many worthy events did you observe but never report? *Alf York.*

(*opposite*) **Another Birkenhead '9' but this was one of the conventional engines, complete with smoke deflectors, and that dubious coat of filth! No.92103 had moved to 8H in April 1965 from Leicester and in this 17th July 1965 view the engine sits out in the typically summer shower waiting to work back home. Note the profusion of gas lamps along the outside of the gable; electricity was yet to reach Yorkshire, apparently.** *N.W.Skinner (ARPT).* (*opposite, bottom*) **Crewe South engines were also regular visitors to Mirfield as witness this Stanier 5P4F No.42968 stabled circa 1950. Note that filth was not really confined to the latter years of steam.** *K.H.Cockerill (ARPT).*

Something with a difference! This view across the main line shows the Mirfield coaling stage doing its job on Saturday 25th January 1964 but in bringing the stage into focus, the photographer has managed one of those one-in-a-million images with two trains in view and both going in the same direction. Nearest the camera is Rebuilt Patriot No.45531 SIR FREDERICK HARRISON approaching with a 12-coach express (1X38) which may well be a football excursion but not having a fixtures almanac we cannot be totally sure (apparently this was an FA Cup 4th Round weekend; readers please put us out of our misery). Between the 'footex' and the stage is a Liverpool-Hull trans-Pennine unit which is either losing the race with the 7P or winning the encounter? *N.W.Skinner (ARPT).* 43

It turned out to be a works job! When Cl.5 No.44658 broke down far from home in July 1966, the Mirfield shed fitters tried to rectify the problem but alas the job was just beyond their capabilities and was more of a main works job so the '5' was tucked away at the side of the shed next to the snowplough which was not going to be required just yet anyway. A tow to Crewe was certainly required as that works was the only one still overhauling and repairing steam. By 11th September the class leader was installed in the Erecting shop and that was that. However, look at the crudely painted 6G languishing where a shed plate should be fitted. Now No.44658 was at the time of the incident allocated to Warrington's Dallam shed but 6G was Llandudno Junction. Official records put the 4-6-0 still at 8B so what was going on? Another mystery of the period? Was the TARA legend a name or simply goodbye in Northern slang which was spelt the same way? Next, look at the way the connecting rod has been secured to the running plate with some rather 'ropy' looking rope. Now apparently the locomotive and its part all reached Crewe intact but I reckon you would have a hard time trying to pull such a stunt nowadays! The Independent snowplough DE900577 with sister DE900578 resided at Mirfield shortly after the NE Region took over until the day Mirfield depot closed after which the two ploughs were moved to Healey Mills. Note the circular bases for the erstwhile fuel-oil tanks which were laid down at Mirfield – see Wakefield. *N.W.Skinner (ARPT).*

The day the 'Royal Scots' came to Mirfield; No.46117 WELSH GUARDSMAN, with its 56D shed plate affixed, stands in full public gaze from the main line on 29th April 1962. Looking half decent and totally intact, the 7P was one of three 'Royal Scots' which were transferred in from Low Moor during December 1961 – the other two were Nos.46113 CAMERONIAN and 46145 THE DUKE OF WELLINGTON'S REGT. (WEST RIDING) – but which departed to Holbeck in June 1962 for storage and eventual withdrawal. They were to pass this way again in the not too distant future. *C.J.B.Sanderson (ARPT).*

(*above*) A visitor from York – B1 No.61002 IMPALA stables alongside the shed on 29th April 1962. (*below*) Gorton based J94 No.68079 rests at Mirfield on that same Sunday whilst en route to its home shed from a month-long Non-Classified repair at Darlington. *Both C.J.B.Sanderson (ARPT).*

We have to include a WD whenever Mirfield is featured; the shed and the class were synonymous! A proud looking No.90068 stands outside the shed with others of her ilk on Sunday 18th August 1962 just a few months after returning from a general overhaul at Darlington. One of the North British Locomotive Company batch – the works plate is still in situ – this engine was purchased by the LNER and taken into their stock in 1947 becoming No.3068. It ended up at Mirfield on 10th September 1961 on transfer from Low Moor but on 5th January 1964 it moved on to Wakefield. The first of them to be allocated was No.90723 on 20th January 1950. By the end of that summer more than half a dozen were resident and the association continued until the shed closed so that no less than forty-two of them resided here at one time or another, eleven of them more than once. *C.J.B.Sanderson (ARPT).*

Laid-up Class 4 tank locomotives 19th August 1962. (*above*) Ivatt No.42285 had come to Mirfield in March 1956 from Newton Heath but DMUs had taken most of its work and so 1962 was spent in store. It moved on to Low Moor in December. (*below*) Fowler No.42406 arrived at Mirfield in August 1949 but had also fallen foul of the diesel units. It moved on to Wakefield in March 1963. Both engines were condemned in August 1965. *Both C.J.B.Sanderson (ARPT).*

WAKEFIELD 25A, 56A

Wakefield – land of the WD 2-8-0s! This is a section of the shed on Sunday 7th November 1965 with four of the 'Austerities' visible and three of those identified as 90698, 90348, and 90360. The engine shed here was rebuilt by the North Eastern Region in 1956 to a design perpetuated by the LMS and adopted by BR as a standard for straight sheds. Up to 1932 the building which was built in 1893 by the L&YR was altered from a dead-end shed to a through shed so that the yard was enlarged and a mechanical coaling plant provided. *A.Ives (ARPT)*.

This image is included for its historical content; not the pair of ex-Lanky engines but the pair of oil tanks – there was actually three – and the oil heating building along with the gantry to transfer the oil to waiting tenders. The date is 10th September 1950 and the installation at Wakefield was complete and ready for work but the crisis which brought about these radical measures was over. The coal shortage was all but averted and BR went back to normal receiving coal from the collieries rather than oil from refineries! In actuality post-war Britain was all but broken financially and the Government had insufficient foreign exchange to purchase the additional oil estimated to cost £300,000 a year so the scheme was scrapped. Coal quantity had dropped during the early post-war years but more dramatically the quality received by the railways had dropped considerably which caused a problem in that more coal was required to do the same job as a few years previously but then quantity too had dropped. A very difficult situation had arisen which appeared initially to have that oil-fired solution but other matters then came into play. Quite a number of locomotives – the original plan was to convert 1235 – were converted ready to burn oil and dozens of depots throughout the country had been fitted out to dispense the oil. Wakefield was one of the more advanced projects. The LMS planned to convert 485 locomotives including all 175 of the LMS-built 7F 0-8-0s, all the S&D 2-8-0s, all 33 of the Garratts, 16 4F 0-6-0s, five Stanier Cl.5s, and 245 Stanier 8F 2-8-0s. Only twenty-five locomotives were converted before the scheme was scrapped and all except four 7F 0-8-0 were converted back to coal, the 7Fs were scrapped! *K.H.Cockerill (ARPT)*.

Two views of the north end of the shed in 1957 (*above*) shortly after the rebuilding was completed. This aspect reveals the barracks on the left and the coaling plant rising above the admin. section. *Clive Allen (ARPT)*. (*below*) On 17th July 1966. *N.W.Skinner (ARPT)*.

A nice selection of locomotives grace Wakefield yard on 23rd March 1957 with, from left to right, WD No.90413, an unidentified 'Crab', WD No.90406, D49 No.62739 THE BADSWORTH from Scarborough, and Cl.5 No.44695 from Low Moor. *F.W.Hampson (ARPT)*.

A line-up of operational WD 2-8-0s at Wakefield 17th July 1965; there are three engines here Nos.90611, 90361 and 90360 which have all had their top lamp irons removed and fixed to the smokebox door just right of the securing handles. No.90281 still wears the lamp iron on top of the door which was deemed to be an unsafe position if the locomotives were working beneath 25kV a.c. catenary. Only one of the group was a Vulcan engine the others were all North British! Wakefield was home to over a hundred and forty of the 'Austerity' locomotives at various periods and at any one time between late 1949 and 1966 there would be fifty or so allocated to the depot. So, we make no apologies if they keep cropping up in these pages. *N.W.Skinner (ARPT).*

The view from beneath the coaling plant on 18th March 1967! To the left is the double-fronted ash plant which was commissioned in 1932 along with the coaler. This end of the yard was all virgin territory up to about 1930 but since then the Wakefield motive power has utilised the area thoroughly. WD No.90407 and a Stanier 8F have business at the ash pit whilst just in line with the second upright can be seen laid-up WD 2-8-0s. Further to the right is a line of empty wagons which had served the coaling plant recently. Above the photographer the huge concrete box forming the coaling plant is slowly deteriorating as the concrete is spalling – it's only been in use for thirty-odd years and already signs of decay are everywhere. Perhaps the forthcoming closure of the depot is a good omen considering the 300 tons of coal in the hoppers along with the weight of the structure itself, along with the machinery in the engine room, combined with a bit of subsidence from the colliery working surrounding the depot might all have conspired to create a spectacular and inconvenient collapse! *Ken Groundwater (ARPT).*

(*opposite*) Wakefield's coaling plant and adjacent ash plant on a quiet Saturday 18th March 1967. The depot closed from 3rd June 1967 and stabled diesel locomotives for a while before becoming a wagon repair shop, that new roof from 1955 coming into its own.
54 *Ken Groundwater (ARPT).*

They were desperate for motive power sometimes at Wakefield but never this desperate. Newton Heath based 'Crab' No.42701 stands out in the yard with its rear coupled wheelset removed. Though undated, the 2-6-0 transferred from Newton Heath to Gorton in July 1963. Wakefield's fitters would have been comfortable sorting out this engine as Wakefield had been home to a few of these 'crab' in the past. As for axle-box jobs, well that was second nature as they had fifty-seven of the 7F 0-8-0 'Austin Sevens' allocated in April 1944. No wonder the WD 2-8-0s were welcomed with open arms! *John Pedelty.*

Again, no date but Peppercorn A1 No.60133 POMMERN was an Ardsley engine from 6th September 1954 until condemned on 21st June 1965. There could be a list of reasons why it was visiting Wakefield – Ardsley coaler out of commission; shed being worked on; etc. – but the date is early 60s' – ATC fitted, electrification warning signs – so the second reason is probably nulled. Someone will know so please let us know too. *John Pedelty.*

A group of visiting enthusiasts form a semi-pose alongside WD No.90091 on an unknown date probably towards the end. If any of them had been aware of the large lump of coal above their heads they might have chosen somewhere else to do the group photo. 90091 was a Goole engine and remained active until 24th June 1967. Were you in that group of spotters? *V.Wake*.

Some damage has taken place with this image but nevertheless it reveals an aspect of Wakefield engine shed we have yet to see. The group of locomotives alongside the shed are mainly former Lancashire & Yorkshire steeds which are in store awaiting the summer timetable and an increase in traffic. Rebuilt 'A' class No.52154 was to plod on for another eleven years and was finally condemned whilst working at Goole shed in November 1960. Sister No.52433 was one of the un-rebuilt members and was an early casualty of the BR withdrawal programme being condemned in September 1961. Others in the line were 2-4-2Ts Nos.10748 and 10755 minus shed plates! The date is 24th April 1949 and 25A is still covered by its original northlight roof although over the years the slates in some areas have been replaced by corrugated materials. It was to be another six years before the money was available to renew the whole roof. The concrete pad is part of the coaling plant approaches where full coal wagons were brought by hand and gravity down to the lifting device which hoisted wagons aloft to tip their contents into a choice of bunkers. Once the wagon was discharged and returned to ground level, it was again allowed to continue its journey by gravity to a siding beyond the coaler - see page 54 - from where it was later returned to a colliery. *K.H.Cockerill (ARPT).*

It's another of those Fowler Cl.4 tanks with enclosed cab again. No.42406 stables in the south yard on 8th September 1963 in amongst the usual residents. In March 1946 a number of these capable locomotives were transferred from Newton Heath shed to three depots in the West Riding – Farnley Junction, Huddersfield, and Mirfield – where they were to spend the rest of their operational lives. No.42406 arrived at Farnley Junction in 1946 and then a year later moved to Low Moor. In August 1949 it transferred to Mirfield – see also page 48 – and then Wakefield in June 1963 where it managed to find some work which was lacking at 56D. However, time caught up with the 2-6-4T and in August 1965 it was condemned. One of its sisters which went to and remained at Huddersfield was operational until September 1966. Behind is the Wakefield enginemens' barracks, one of the largest on the old LMS system. *N.W.Skinner (ARPT)*.

Bank Hall 'Jubilee' No.45719 GLORIOUS is prepared for its journey home on 14th June 1958. Note the Fowler high sided tender No.4573 which was coupled during an overhaul in April 1957; the 6P eventually got a Stanier tender, its first – No.10093 – in November 1958. *C.J.B.Sanderson (ARPT).*

Here's one for a polo – see later! WD No.90112 has just returned from Darlington works after a Heavy General overhaul which was completed on 27th May 1961. It is now 17th June and the 2-8-0 has been thoroughly run-in by Darlington shed and the 8F is certainly ready for a few more years work before requiring works attention again. This engine was one of those which started its civilian career on the GWR at Oxley in May 1947 but after working from eight other depots – mainly on the LM region – it arrived at 56A in June 1958. Behind the WD and in fact dominating the background was the fairly new Wakefield 'B' power station which was commissioned in 1957 and was rated at 234 megawatts net capacity. *C.J.B.Sanderson (ARPT).*

It always bothered me that the V2s were never coupled to 8-wheel tenders – those six-wheel jobs just didn't look right. However, that would have been the last thing on this V2s mind if it was able. No.60861 was stored at Wakefield on 19th August 1962 and had been laid-up for some time by appearances. It was transferred to Wakefield from Ardsley on 10th September 1961 and did little work. On 25th November 1962 it was sent back to Ardsley when 56A had a clear-out; the Stanier Cl.3 behind, No.40147 was condemned and sent to Crewe for the necessary! Meanwhile Ardsley could find little use for the V2 and so, on 12th August 1963 it was condemned and then taken into the works at Doncaster on 22nd August for scrapping. This little gathering was in the south-east corner of the shed yard. *C.J.B.Sanderson (ARPT)*.

This view of the interior of Wakefield shed on the 5th May 1957 reveals the near new condition of the roof and the smoke ducting over each road. The work had been completed in May 1955 to a standard BR design using post-stressed, pre-cast concrete main beams each spanning four tracks; the beams were constructed on site and craned into position when sufficient were ready. The cross section of these beams was 36 inches high and 18 inches wide with a span of 64 feet. They were placed at 24ft centres and longitudinal secondary pre-stressed beams of channel section, placed in pairs, were laid on them to carry the roof cladding. The smoke ducts are continuous and suspended from the roof but in the event of the shed being used later by diesel or electric motive power the ducting can be removed without any alteration to the fabric of the roof; the uptakes built into the roof would be left in situ to form natural ventilation. From the new to the old and they didn't come much older than the six-coupled locomotive taking centre-stage here. L&YR 2F 0-6-0 No.52044 was a Barton Wright F15 class dating from 1887 and built by Beyer, Peacock, Manchester. The locomotive has been preserved and now works on the K&WVR. However, sister engine No.52016 which was the penultimate member of the class and which worked at Patricroft shed in Manchester should have been the last one but it had a premature withdrawal after an unfortunate accident on the shed yard at Patricroft when a WD 2-8-0 ran into the ex-Lanky 0-6-0 in October 1956 and basically wrote it off! The WD, which lived to fight another day, was from Wakefield! *John Phillips-Alan Bowman collection.*

When the Dub-Dees ruled at 56A! This undated view taken at the south end of the shed shows WD 2-8-0s everywhere. This end of the shed is the section which was opened out in 1932 and it will be noted that the curtain wall is different from that spanning the north end, also the rolled steel joists and beams supporting the brickwork are only found at this end. The northern end has just precast concrete segments. Back to the engines, and No.90404 spent the whole of its BR life allocated to Wakefield except for a fortnight spanning January and February 1956 when Goole required its services. Arriving from overhaul at Crewe – Casual Heavy 30th June to 5th August 1949 – on 13th August 1949 after WD storage, the 2-8-0 worked from Wakefield until withdrawn on 3rd June 1967. After languishing at 56A for seven months, No.90404 was towed away to Hull where an infamous scrap yard awaited in late February 1968 to despatch the 8F. Wakefield sent forty of her original stud to Hull for breaking. *Ken Groundwater (ARPT).*

And now we present this nice cab-side image of WD No.90415 on 3rd April 1965. The O beneath the number was a curiosity of Wakefield shed and was known as a Polo – the likeness to a popular mint confectionery being apparent – and was applied to the cabsides of any WD which was recently ex-works or was in good mechanical condition. These locomotives were then used on the arduous Dearne Valley coal train duties where trip working along with associated bonuses and timings were crucial; the 40 m.p.h. design speed of the WD 2-8-0s was often called upon to fulfil the workings. At any one time 56A would have about twenty of their WD fleet available for the Dearne Valley jobs. Of course there came a time in each locomotive's life when it could no longer perform and that was when the black paint came out! *A.Ives (ARPT)*.

This image has been included to illustrate the former coaling stage at Wakefield which was one of the largest such structures on BR. The passing A3 on a lightweight working is – apparently – No.60064 TAGALIE and the date is 17th June 1961. North Eastern Region cleaning standards have sunk to a new low. *C.J.B.Sanderson (ARPT).*

NORMANTON - Again!

As promised, we present more on Normanton but alas we can only fit one image into the album. This angle of the depot is unusual and shows 9F No.92172 – un-adopted it appears – on the outer road of the shed on 7th November 1965, a Sunday with signals pegged awaiting the meagre traffic. The 9F was one of Doncaster's lot received in early 1958 and hardly used. It was withdrawn during the April following this encounter. From this aspect we can see the timber baulks shoring up the shed's gable end wall. *A.Ives (ARPT)*

ROYSTON 20C, 55D

This image is included for the modellers who are now becoming a rather precise bunch demanding illustrative proof of any changes from the norm concerning locomotives and indeed rolling stock, not to mention the buildings too. The date is 7th November 1965 and resident 8F No.48281 – it was withdrawn at Royston – is wearing one of those stars which announced to all and sundry that they were balanced. It was the position of the star and the size of those figures which caught my attention. The 2-8-0 had received a heavy overhaul at Darlington during the previous winter hence those numbers and that star placing; the actual balancing work had taken place at a LMR workshop a few years beforehand. *A.Ives (ARPT)*.

This image serves two purposes: Firstly that ex-LNER locomotives – I know we're stretching the LNER bit – were regular visitors to Royston as witness York based Thompson B1 No.61303 (actually built 26th March 1948) stabled alongside the second point, a BR Sulzer Type 2 diesel electric locomotive which was looking as filthy as the surrounding steam locomotives. Type 1s, 2s, 3s and the occasional Type 4 stabled at Royston having mainly worked up from Toton, or Tinsley. This scene was recorded on a typical dank 7th November in 1965. *A.Ives (ARPT).*

A line-up outside the shed on 17th July 1966 with WD No.90615, and Stanier 8Fs Nos.48763 and 48177 all identified. The 'Austerity' has a roughly painted – who did they use to apply these figures? – 55D where a shed plate should be affixed whilst another chalked 55D has been put onto the bufferbeam. However, look at the 56A shed plate on the bottom of said beam. To clear up any doubts, No.90615 had been a Wakefield engine since 23rd September 1949 but had transferred to Royston on 18th June 1966 so we can forgive the temporary arrangements as the 2-8-0 had only been at 55D for a month and it appears that the 56A plate was riveted on anyway! To spoil the party No.90615 moved on to Normanton on 28th January 1967 from where it was 'officially' withdrawn on 16th September. The 56A plate had been removed by Friday 29th September nearly two weeks after the engine was withdrawn but the WD was still active then and remained so until Sunday 1st October; Normanton closed the following day. As an aside, No.90615's numberplate had also been removed but a neatly painted 55E had replaced that clumsy 55D. At the end of the row of locomotives is a diesel fuel oil tank in its bund-wall and a sure sign that the depot had an allocation of or dealt with diesel locomotives. At the time of this photograph, Royston had seven of the ubiquitous BR 350 h.p. 0-6-0DE shunters on the books: D3294, D3377, D3378, D3379, D3458, D3937, and D3941. The original seven, D3375 to D3381 had come here new from Derby during August and September 1957 but had mainly dispersed and replaced by others; it was an on-going process with a dozen of them involved before the depot eventually closed. N.W.Skinner (ARPT).

71

All ten roads of the Royston engine shed on 17th July 1966 virtually unchanged since the depot was opened by the LMS on 17th March 1932. The design of the roof reflects the then lightweight covering adopted by the LMS for their re-roofing projects of certain existing sheds such as Birkenhead, Crewe South, Edge Hill, and Stockport Edgeley for instance during that pre-war decade. Besides the standard roof, Royston was equipped with that small coaling plant but just as important was the turning triangle – the apex of which was to the right – and which did away with the requirement of a turntable. Admitted Royston had the room available which many inner-city depots did not and so the LMS took full advantage of that situation (in actuality the subsidence in this area would have made a turntable something of a white-elephant because it would have been inoperable within a few years if not sooner). Built on the east side of the former Midland Railway main line south of Wakefield, the depot was located right in the middle of what might be conceived as 'coal country' when in fact it was then just another engine shed situated in one of the United Kingdom's numerous coalfields. It's worth stating that what we are looking at here is now total history. A glimpse of a past when Britain was virtually self-sufficient and self-sustaining as regards fuel and power! Admitted the air quality around Royston was not the best in the country with the coke ovens and coal by-products plants at Monkton seen in the left background adding a rather pungent odour along with various unseen pollutants beside those which were more visible. The hillock on the right was also a man-made monument to industry being the end product of the spoil lifted out of the earth during the decades of man's search for the 'black gold' which is now looked upon in disdain as a major source of poison inflicted upon the planet – what's next in the eco warriors sights? Back to our subject, it can be seen that besides the WD 2-8-0s and the solitary 350 h.p. 0-6-0DE shunter, all the locomotives are of LMS origin. *N.W.Skinner (ARPT).*

We saw Stanier Cl.3 No.40181 in dire straits at Normanton shed on pages 78 and 79 of Leeds Engine Sheds Pt.1. Here she is at Royston on 8th May 1960 when she was still operational, virtually ex-works, and wanted! *N.W.Skinner (ARPT)*.

WD 2-8-0 No.90591 had arrived at Royston on 25th March 1962 on transfer from Huddersfield but on 12th November that same year the 'Austerity' had been condemned and became one of only six of the class withdrawn at Royston. This is the engine six days later on a damp 18th November 1962 complete with covered chimney, and all the relevant plates. No.90591 was eventually hauled away to the BR works at Darlington where it was cut up during August 1963. *Raymond Embleton*.

A view of the shed yard from the main line embankment 8th May 1960; besides the 'stored pending withdrawal' locomotives on this nearest track, the rest of the track work beyond was in continuous use: The nearer of the steel-framed buildings was the coaling plant which when supplied in 1932 was a 'state-of-the-art' small to medium size mechanical coaling plant with a below-ground storage hopper fed by tipping the contents of whole wagons. The coal was 'on-demand' for each locomotive and a system of small buckets connected by conveyor carried their contents to the top of the plant where it was discharged onto a chute thence into the waiting locomotive. A similar contraption was in use at Carlisle's Upperby shed. Further down the yard is the depot's ash plant - topped with a control housing complete with a pitched roof - which was a single skip lifting appliance which lifted a skip bucket from its normal below-ground location when it was full of ash and clinker tipped from narrow gauge tubs in both the ash pit and alongside at ground level. The 2P 4-4-0 No.40581 was languishing here awaiting the call to the scrapyard which would come in September. The engine had been at Royston since October 1957 – having relieved another – working a singular duty only suited to the large-wheeled 4-4-0s but now apparently superfluous. *N.W.Skinner (ARPT).*

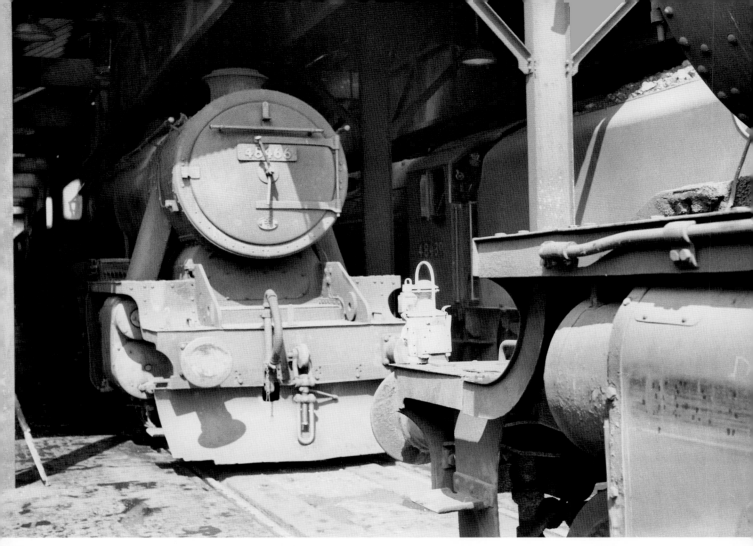

Resident 8F No.48466 with sister No.48439 on its left side, shelter inside the shed on Sunday 17th July 1966. By this time the number of Stanier 8Fs allocated to 55D was falling with less than twenty now operational although the WD 2-8-0 fleet numbers allocated to Royston had risen to eleven from none in early March 1959 when the first example arrived and the ex-LMS 8Fs numbered twenty-five. Perhaps the influence of nearby Wakefield was beginning to tell? Altogether some twenty-nine WD 2-8-0s served Royston during that eight year period of the depot's existence whereas the Stanier 2-8-0s numbered seventy-seven engines over that longer period from their introduction. Many engines came new from various LMS workshops whilst others – Swindon-built examples for instance – used Royston as their first LMS port-of-call after being released from the Great Western to the LMS. Likewise, ex-LNER built engines used Royston as their first LMS depot after release from LNER stewardship. Of course many ended their days at Royston with no less than thirty-four of them being withdrawn at the depot. *N.W.Skinner (ARPT)*.

Another view of Royston shed and part of its locomotive stud on that Sunday in July 1966. Ivatt Class 4 No.43076 stands proud of the shed over one of the preparation pits with Westhouses based 8F No.48177 in a similar situation alongside. The Cl.4 had transferred into Royston during the previous October – its first move – from Hull Dairycoates where it started its career in October 1950. Note that Royston fitted one of their 55D shed plates but did not bother removing the (Hull) Dairycoates legend painted on the bufferbeam; I wonder if it remained until withdrawal? The end came fairly quickly for the 2-6-0 when in June 1967 it was transferred to Holbeck then in August to Low Moor. It was condemned in September at the Bradford depot. Now, what job did that small P large 62 target board represent? As an aside, remember sister No.43072 which ran away on a goods train at Laisterdyke on 10th November 1964 and ended up smashing through the parapet of the retaining wall alongside the former Great Northern Railway passenger terminus at Adolphus Street in Bradford, falling 30ft into Dryden Street below and ended up being cut up on site by Laisterdyke scrap merchant G.W. Butler? There were no injuries! Happy days! *N.W.Skinner (ARPT).*

An unusual visitor from the Western Lines in the shape of ex-LNWR G2a 0-8-0 No.49180. From which direction the 7F arrived in this part of the West Riding is unknown as is the reason why one of the class should work over from its home shed at Crewe South; an assumption would bring it to Huddersfield via Stockport and 55G would have used it on a local job to Royston. The date is 11th May 1958 and the 0-8-0 is not too far from being withdrawn – March 1959 – and its external appearance has all the hallmarks of neglect. Some forty-six years old by this date, the 7F was one of more than five hundred such 0-8-0s which reached Nationalisation surely a tribute to their original robust design and performance. The identity of the 8F 2-8-0 remains a mystery. *Gordon Turner/GD/ARPT*.

We can't leave Royston without mention of their ex-LMS 4F 0-6-0s which were fixtures at the depot from its opening to – virtually – closure. In September 1935 just three months after the first Stanier 8Fs had been put into traffic at Toton, Royston shed had eight 4F 0-6-0s allocated as against eighteen 3Fs, four 2Fs, six 3F 0-6-0Ts, and five 7F 0-8-0s which totalled at forty and which was a far cry from post-war numbers which passed half as many again. In May 1944 some fifty-four engines were allocated and one of the War Department 2-10-0s – No.3666 – was on loan. The breakdown of types was ten 4F 0-6-0s, ten 3F 0-6-0s, three 2F 0-6-0s, five 3F 0-6-0Ts, four 5MT 2-6-0s, seven 8F 2-8-0s, three Cl.3 2-6-2Ts, two 2P 4-4-0s, two 4P 4-4-0s, three Cl.4 2-6-4Ts, three 1P 0-4-4Ts, one 2P 2-4-2T, and no 7F 0-8-0s! By the end of the LMS the 4Fs were down to five whilst Stanier 8F amounted to twenty-five. Those 4F numbers remained somewhat stable throughout the BR period so that by the end of the 1965 summer the following were still on the books 43906, 43968, 43983, 44056, and 44446. They all went in 1965 as follows August 43983, October 44056, November 43906 and 44446, December 43968. This is No.44056 on 7th November 1965 in that siding alongside the main line. Others were there too: 43906, 43968 (not yet withdrawn). The others had gone! This aspect of 44056 shows off nicely the tender provided with covers for the coal space for when the locomotive was on snow plough duties; the sliding cover is now in the open position. *A.Ives (ARPT)*.